CROCHE

Decorative Doilies™

By Diane Stone

General Information

Many of the products used in this pattern book can be purchased from local craft, fabric and variety stores, or from the Annie's Attic Needlecraft Catalog (see Customer Service information on page 16).

Contents

Simply White 2

Heart's Desire 4

Pineapple Rose 6

Christmas Rose 8

Sunflowers 10

Daisies 12

Lilacs & Lace 13

Stitch Guide 15

SKILL LEVEL

INTERMEDIATE

FINISHED SIZE

11½ inches across

MATERIALS

- ❏ Crochet cotton size 10:
  200 yds white
- ❏ 30 yds silver lamé thread
- ❏ Size 7/1.65mm steel crochet
  hook or size needed to
  obtain gauge
- ❏ Sewing needle
- ❏ Sewing thread
- ❏ 12 white size 6mm
  pearl beads

GAUGE

Rnds 1–3 = 2 inches

SPECIAL STITCHES

Beginning popcorn (beg pc):
Ch 4, 4 tr in same st, drop lp from hook, insert hook in top of ch-4, pull dropped lp through.

Popcorn (pc): 5 tr in next st or ch sp, drop lp from hook insert hook in top of first tr of group, pull dropped lp through.

Picot: Ch 6, sc in 3rd ch from hook, hdc in next ch, ch 2.

INSTRUCTIONS

DOILY

Rnd 1: With white, wrap thread around finger twice to form a ring, ch 3 *(counts as first dc)*, 15 dc in ring, pull thread tightly to close ring, join with sl st in top of ch-3. *(16 dc)*

Rnd 2: Ch 3, dc in same st, 2 dc in each st around, join. *(32 dc)*

Rnd 3: Ch 3, 2 dc in next st, [dc in next st, 2 dc in next st] around, join. *(48 dc)*

Rnd 4: Ch 3, dc in next st, 2 dc in next st, [dc in each of next 2 sts, 2 dc in next st] around, join. *(64 dc)*

Rnd 5: Ch 3, dc in each of next 2 sts, 2 dc in next st, [dc in each of next 3 sts, 2 dc in next st] around, join. *(80 dc)*

Rnd 6: Working in **back lps** *(see Stitch Guide)*, ch 3, dc in each of next 3 sts, 2 dc in next st, [dc in each of next 4 sts, 2 dc in next st] around, join. *(96 dc)*

Rnd 7: Ch 1, sc in first st, [ch 3, sk next st, sc in next st] around, join with dc in beg sc forming last ch sp.

Rnd 8: Ch 1, sc in last ch sp made, [ch 3, sc in next ch sp] around, join with dc in beg sc.

Rnds 9 & 10: Ch 1, sc in last ch sp made, [ch 4, sc in next ch sp] around, join with ch 1, dc in beg sc.

Rnd 11: Ch 1, sc in last ch sp made, [ch 5, sc in next ch sp] around, join with ch 2, dc in beg sc.

Rnd 12: Ch 1, sc in last ch sp made, ch 5, [sc in next ch sp, ch 5] around, join with sl st in beg sc. Fasten off.

FIRST FLOWER MOTIF

Rnd 1: Form a ring with white, ch 1, 8 sc in ring, pull thread tightly to close ring, join with sl st in beg sc. *(8 sc)*

Petals

Rnd 2: Beg pc *(see Special Stitches)* in first st, [ch 5, **pc** *(see Special Stitches)* in next st] around, join with ch 2, dc in top of beg pc forming last ch sp.

Rnd 3: Ch 1, (sc, ch 3, sc) in last ch sp made, ch 2, sc in any ch-5 sp on last rnd of Doily, ch 2, [(sc, ch 3, sc) in center ch of next ch sp on Flower Motif, ch 5] around, join with sl st in beg sc. Fasten off.

JOINED FLOWER MOTIF
Make 10.

Rnds 1 & 2: Work same as rnds 1 and 2 of First Flower Motif.

Rnd 3: Ch 1, (sc, ch 3, sc) in last ch sp made, ch 2, sk next 3 ch sps on last rnd of Doily, sc in next ch-5 sp on Doily, ch 2, (sc, ch 3, sc) in center ch of next ch sp on this Motif, ch 5, (sc, ch 3, sc) in next ch sp, ch 2, sc in corresponding ch-5 sp on last Flower Motif, ch 2, [(sc, ch 3, sc) in center ch of next ch sp on this Motif, ch 5] around, join with sl st in beg sc. Fasten off.

LAST FLOWER MOTIF
Rnds 1 & 2: Work same as rnds 1 and 2 of First Flower Motif.
Rnd 3: Ch 1, (sc, ch 3, sc) in last ch sp made, ch 2, sk next 3 ch sps on last rnd of Doily, sc in next ch 5 sp on Doily, ch 2, (sc, ch 3, sc) in center ch of next ch sp on this motif, ch 5, (sc, ch 3, sc) in center ch of next ch sp, ch 2, sc in corresponding ch-5 sp on last Flower Motif, ch 2, [(sc, ch 3, sc) in center ch of next ch sp on Flower Motif, ch 5] 3 times, (sc, ch 3, sc) in center ch of next ch sp, ch 2, sc in corresponding ch sp of First Flower Motif, ch 2, (sc, ch 3, sc) in center ch of next ch sp, ch 5, join with sl st in beg sc. Fasten off.

EDGING
Working in unworked ch-5 sps around outer edge, join with sc in first ch-5 sp to left of side joining, ch 3, sc in same ch sp, *[**picot** *(see Special Stitches)*, (sc, ch 3, sc) in center ch of next ch-5 sp] twice, ch 8, sc in 2nd ch from hook, hdc in next ch, dc in next ch, ch 3**, (sc, ch 3, sc) in center ch of next ch-5 sp on next Flower Motif, rep from * around, ending last rep at **, join with sl st in beg sc. Fasten off.

Sew 1 bead to center of each Flower Motif.

FILL-IN
Working in the 3 sk ch-5 sps on last rnd of Doily between Flower Motifs, join with sc in center ch of first ch-5 sp, (dc, ch 3, sl st in top of last dc just made, ch 1) 3 times in center ch of next ch-5 sp, sc in center ch of last ch-5 sp. Fasten off.

Work in each sp between Flower Motifs.

RUFFLE
Rnd 1: Working in **front lps** *(see Stitch Guide)* of rnd 5 on Doily, join with sl st in any st, ch 4 *(counts as dc and ch 1)*, (dc, ch 1, dc) in next st, ch 1, [dc in next st, ch 1, (dc, ch 1, dc) in next st, ch 1] around, join with sl st in 3rd ch of beg ch-4. *(120 dc)*
Rnd 2: Ch 5 *(counts as first tr and ch 1)*, [tr in next st, ch 1] around, join with sl st in 4th ch of beg ch-5. Fasten off.
Rnd 3: Join silver lamé thread with sc in any ch sp, ch 4, [sc in next ch sp, ch 4] around, join with sl st in beg sc. Fasten off. ❑❑

Heart's Desire

FINISHED SIZE
13 inches across

MATERIALS
- ❑ Crochet cotton size 10:
  - 200 yds ecru
  - 75 yds red
- ❑ Size 6/1.80mm steel crochet hook or size needed to obtain gauge

GAUGE
Rnds 1–3 = 2 inches

SPECIAL STITCH
Cluster (cl): *Yo twice, insert hook in ring, yo, pull lp through, [yo, pull through 2 lps on hook] twice, rep from * twice, yo, pull through all lps on hook.

INSTRUCTIONS

HEART
Make 12.

Rnd 1: With red, wrap thread around finger twice to form a ring, ch 6, [**cl** *(see Special Stitch)*, ch 5] twice, cl, ch 6, sl st in ring, pull end of thread to tighten ring, **do not join.** *(3 cls)*

Rnd 2: Ch 1, working in chs of ch-6, sc in first ch, ch 2, [dc in next ch, ch 2] 5 times, sk next cl, [dc in next ch, ch 3, sk next ch] twice, dc in next ch, ch 1, (dc, ch 2, tr, ch 2, dc) in top of next cl, ch 1, [dc in next ch, ch 2, sk next ch] twice, dc in next ch, sk next cl, ch 2, [dc in next ch, ch 2] 5 times, ch 2, sc in last ch, sl st in ring. Fasten off.
Lay Hearts aside to be joined later.

DOILY
Rnd 1: With ecru, wrap thread around finger twice to form a ring, thread, ch 3 *(counts as first dc)*, 15 dc in ring, pull thread tightly to close ring, join with sl st in top of ch-3. *(16 dc)*

Rnd 2: Ch 3, dc in same st, 2 dc in each st around, join. *(32 dc)*

Rnd 3: Ch 3, 2 dc in next st, [dc in next st, 2 dc in next st] around, join. *(48 dc)*

Rnd 4: Ch 3, dc in next st, 2 dc in next st, [dc in each of next 2 sts, 2 dc in next st] around, join. *(64 dc)*

Rnd 5: Ch 3, dc in each of next 2 sts, 2 dc in next st, [dc in each of next 3 sts, 2 dc in next st] around, join. *(80 dc)*

Rnd 6: Working in **back lps** *(see Stitch Guide)*, ch 3, dc in each of next 3 sts, 2 dc in next st, [dc in each of next 4 sts, 2 dc in next st] around, join. *(96 dc)*

Rnd 7: Ch 1, sc in first st, [ch 3, sk next st, sc in next st] around, join with dc in beg sc forming last ch sp.

Rnd 8: Ch 1, sc in last ch sp made, [ch 3, sc in next ch sp] around, join with sl st in beg sc.

Rnd 9: Sl st in first ch sp, ch 3, dc in same ch sp, ch 1, [2 dc in next ch sp, ch 1] around, join with sl st in top of ch-3.

Rnd 10: Sl st to ch sp, ch 1, sc in ch sp, [ch 4, sc in next ch sp] around, join with ch 1, dc in beg sc to form last ch sp.

Rnd 11: Ch 1, sc in last ch sp made, [ch 5, sc in next ch sp] around, join with ch 2, dc in beg sc.

Rnd 12: Ch 1, sc in last ch sp formed, ch 5, [sc in next ch sp, ch 5] around, join with sl st in beg sc. Fasten off.

JOINING
First Heart
With RS of Heart facing, join ecru with sc in 2nd ch-2 sp on left side of Heart, [ch 4, sc in next ch-2 sp] 3 times, ch 5, sc in next ch-2 sp, [ch 4, sc in next ch-2 sp] 4 times, ch 2, sc in any ch-5 sp on last rnd of Doily, ch 2, sc

in next ch-2 sp on Heart, [ch 4, sc in next ch sp on Heart] 4 times, ch 5, sc in next ch-2 sp, [ch 4, sc in next ch 2 sp] 3 times, ch 7, join with sl st in beg sc. Fasten off.

Next Heart
Join 10.

With RS of Heart facing, join ecru with sc in 2nd ch-2 sp on left side of Heart, [ch 4, sc in next ch-2 sp] 3 times, ch 5, sc in next ch-2 sp, [ch 4, sc in next ch-2 sp] 4 times, ch 2, sk next 3 ch sps to left of joining of last Heart to Doily, sc in next ch-5 sp on Doily, ch 2, sc in next ch-2 sp on Heart, [ch 4, sc in next ch sp on heart] 4 times, ch 2, sc in corresponding ch-5 sp of last Heart, ch 2, sc in next ch-2 sp on this Heart, [ch 4, sc in next ch 2 sp] 3 times, ch 7, join with sl st in beg sc. Fasten off.

Last Heart

With RS of Heart facing, join ecru with sc in 2nd ch-2 sp on left side of Heart, [ch 4, sc in next ch-2 sp] 3 times, ch 2, sc in corresponding ch-5 sp of First Heart, ch 2, sc in next ch-2 sp on this Heart, [ch 4, sc in next ch-2 sp] 4 times, ch 2, sk next 3 ch-5 sps on Doily, sc in corresponding ch-5 sp on last rnd of Doily, ch 2, sc in next ch-2 sp on Heart, [ch 4, sc in next ch sp on Heart] 4 times, ch 2, sc in corresponding ch-5 sp of last Heart, ch 2, sc in next ch-2 sp on this Heart, [ch 4, sc in next ch 2 sp] 3 times, ch 7, join with sl st in beg sc. Fasten off.

EDGING

Rnd 1: Join ecru with sl st in 3rd ch-4 sp on the left side of Heart, *ch 3, sc in next ch-4 sp on next Heart, [ch 5, sc in next ch sp] twice, ch 5, (2 dc, ch 2, 2 dc) in center ch of ch-7**, [ch 5, sc in next ch-4 sp] 3 times, rep from * around, ending last rep at **, [ch 5, sc in next ch-4 sp] twice, join with ch 2, dc in beg sc to form last ch sp.

Rnd 2: Ch 1, sc in ch sp just made, *ch 3, sk next ch-3 sp, sc in next ch-5 sp, [ch 5, (sc, ch 3, sc) in next ch sp] twice, ch 5, (2 dc, ch 2, 2 dc) in next ch-2 sp, [ch 5, (sc, ch 3, sc) in next ch sp] twice**, ch 5, sc in next ch sp, rep from * around, ending last rep at **, join with ch 2, dc in beg sc.

Rnd 3: Ch 1, sc in last ch sp made, *ch 3, sk next ch-3 sp, sc in next ch-5 sp, ch 5, (sc, ch 5, sc) in next ch-5 sp, ch 5, sc in next ch-5 sp, 8 dc in next ch-2 sp, sc in next ch-5 sp, ch 5, (sc, ch 3, sc) in next ch-5 sp, ch 5**, sc in next ch-5 sp, rep from * around, ending last rep at **, join with sl st in beg sc. Fasten off.

RUFFLE

Rnd 1: Working in **front lps** (see Stitch Guide) of rnd 5 on Doily, join ecru with sl st in any st, ch 5 (counts as tr and ch 1), (tr, ch 1, tr) in next st, ch 1, [tr in next st, ch 1, (tr, ch 1, tr) in next st, ch 1] around, join with sl st in 4th ch of beg ch-5. (120 tr)

Rnd 2: Ch 5, [tr in next st, ch 1] around, join with sl st in 4th ch of beg ch-5. Fasten off.

Rnd 3: Join red with sc in any ch sp, ch 4, [sc in next ch sp, ch 4] around, join with sl st in beg sc. Fasten off. ❏❏

Pineapple Rose

SKILL LEVEL

INTERMEDIATE

FINISHED SIZE
13 Inches across

MATERIALS
- ❏ Crochet cotton size 10:
    200 yds ecru
    100 yds dark yellow
    100 yds light yellow
    50 yds light green
- ❏ Size 6/1.80mm steel crochet hook or size needed to obtain gauge

GAUGE
Rnds 1–3 = 2 inches

SPECIAL STITCHES

Beginning popcorn (beg pc): Ch 3 *(counts as first dc)*, 3 dc in same st or ch sp, drop lp from hook, insert hook in top of ch 3, pull dropped lp through.

Popcorn (pc): 4 dc in st or ch sp, drop lp from hook, insert hook in first dc of group, pull dropped lp through.

Shell: (2 dc, ch 2, 2 dc) in next ch sp.

Picot: Ch 3, sl st in 2nd ch from hook.

INSTRUCTIONS
DOILY

Rnd 1: With ecru, wrap thread around finger twice to form a ring, ch 3 *(counts as dc)*, 15 dc in ring, pull end of thread tightly to close ring, join with sl st in top of beg ch-3. *(16 dc)*

Rnd 2: Ch 3, dc in same st, 2 dc in each st around, join. *(32 dc)*

Rnd 3: Ch 3, 2 dc in next st, [dc in next st, 2 dc in next st] around, join. *(48 dc)*

Rnd 4: Ch 3, dc in next st, 2 dc in next st, [dc in each of next 2 sts, 2 dc in next st] around, join. *(64 dc)*

Rnd 5: Working in **back lps** *(see Stitch Guide)*, ch 3, dc in each of next 2 sts, 2 dc in next st, [dc in each of next 3 sts, 2 dc in next st] around, join. *(80 dc)*

Rnd 6: Ch 3, dc in each of next 2 sts, 2 dc in next st, [dc in each of next 3 sts, 2 dc in next st] around, join. *(96 dc)*

Rnd 7: Ch 3, dc in each of next 2 sts, 2 dc in next st, [dc in each of next 3 sts, 2 dc in next st] around, join. *(120 dc)*

Rnd 8: Ch 3, dc in each of next 3 sts, 2 dc in next st, [dc in each of next 4 sts, 2 dc in next st] around, join. *(144 dc)*

Rnd 9: Ch 1, sc in first st, [ch 4, sk next 2 dc, sc in next st] around, sk last st, join with ch 1, dc in beg sc forming last ch sp. *(48 ch sps)*

Rnd 10: Ch 1, sc in ch sp last made, [ch 5, sc in next ch sp] around, join with ch 2, dc in beg sc forming last ch sp.

Rnd 11: Ch 1, sc in last ch sp made, [ch 5, sc in next ch sp] around, join with ch 2, dc in first sc.

Rnd 12: Ch 1, sc in last ch sp made, [ch 5, sc in next ch sp] around, join with sl st in beg sc.

Rnd 13: Sl st in next ch sp, ch 3 *(counts as first dc)*, 8 dc in same ch sp, *ch 1, **shell** *(see Special Stitches)* in next ch sp, ch 1, sc in next ch sp, ch 5, sc in next ch sp, ch 1, shell in next ch sp, ch 1**, 9 dc in next ch sp, rep from * around, ending last rep at **, join with sl st in top of beg ch-3.

Rnd 14: Beg pc *(see Special Stitches)* in first st, *[ch 1, sk next st, **pc** *(see Special Stitches)* in next st] 4 times, ch 1, sk next ch sp, shell in ch sp of next shell, ch 5, sc in next ch-5 sp, ch 5, shell in ch sp of next shell, ch 1**, pc in next st, rep from * around, ending last rep at **, join with sl st in top of beg pc.

Rnd 15: Sl st in next ch-1 sp, beg pc in same ch sp, *[ch 1, pc in next ch-1 sp] 3 times, ch 1, sk next ch sp, shell in next shell, [ch 5, sc in next ch-5 sp] twice, ch 5, shell in next shell, ch 1, sk next ch-1 sp**, pc in next ch-1 sp, rep from * around, ending last rep at **, join.

Rnd 16: Sl st in next ch-1 sp, beg pc in same ch sp, *[ch 1, pc in next ch-1 sp] twice, ch 1, sk next ch sp, shell in next shell, [ch 5, sc in next ch sp] 3 times, ch 5, shell in next shell, ch 1, sk next ch-1 sp**, pc in next ch-1 sp, rep from * around, ending last rep at **, join.

Rnd 17: Sl st in next ch-1 sp, beg pc in same ch sp, *ch 1, pc in next ch-1 sp, ch 1, sk next ch sp, shell in next shell, [ch 5, sc in next ch sp] 4 times, ch 5, shell in next shell, ch 1, sk next ch-1 sp**, pc in next ch-1 sp, rep from * around, ending last rep at **, join.

Rnd 18: Sl st in next ch-1 sp, beg pc in same ch sp, *ch 1, sk next ch sp, shell in next shell, [ch 5, sc in next ch sp] twice, 2 dc in first ch of next ch sp, [dc in next ch, 2 dc in next ch] twice, [sc in next ch sp, ch 5] twice, shell in next shell, ch 1, sk next ch-1 sp**, pc in next ch-1 sp,

rep from * around, ending last rep at **, join.

Rnd 19: Sl st across to ch sp of next shell, ch 1, sc in ch sp of same shell, [ch 5, sc in next ch sp] twice, ch 5, sk first 3 dc of next dc group, sc in next dc, ch 3, sc in next dc, ch 5, sk last 3 dc, [sc in next ch sp, ch 5] twice, sc in ch sp of next shell, ch 9**, sc in ch sp of next shell, rep from * around, ending last rep at **, join with sl st in beg sc.

Rnd 20: Sl st to center of first ch sp, ch 1, sc in same ch, *ch 5, sc in next ch sp, [sk first ch of next ch-5 sp, 2 dc in next ch, (dc, **picot**—*see Special Stitches*, dc) in next ch, 2 dc in next ch, sk last ch] twice, sc in next ch-5 sp, ch 5, sc in next ch sp, working in chs of next ch-9, [2 dc in next ch, dc in next ch] 4 times, 2 dc in last ch**, sc in next ch sp, rep from * around, ending last rep at **, join. Fasten off.

RUFFLE

Rnd 1: Working in **front lps** *(see Stitch Guide)* of rnd 4 on Doily, holding 1 strand of light yellow and 1 strand dark yellow tog as 1, join with sc in first dc past joining, ch 4, sk next 3 sts, [sc in next st, ch

4, sk next 3 sts] around, join with sl st in beg sc. *(16 ch sps)*

Rnd 2: Sl st in first ch sp, ch 1, (sc, hdc, 4 dc, hdc, sc) in same ch sp and in each ch sp around, **do not join.**

Rnd 3: Ch 1, working behind petals, [sc in next ch-4 sp of rnd 1 between center 2 dc of rnd 2, ch 5] around, join with sl st in beg sc.

Rnd 4: Sl st in next ch sp, ch 1, (sc, hdc, 6 dc, hdc, sc) in same ch sp and in each ch sp around, **do not join.**

Rnd 5: Ch 1, working behind petals just made, [sc in next ch-5 sp on rnd before last between center 2 dc of last rnd, ch 5] around, join with sl st in beg sc.

Rnd 6: Sl st in first ch sp, ch 1, (sc, hdc, 8 dc, hdc, sc) in same ch sp and in each ch sp around, **do not join.**

Rnd 7: Ch 2, *sc in next ch-5 sp on rnd before last between center 2 dc of last rnd, ch 5] around, join with sl st in beg sc. Fasten off.

Rnd 8: Holding 2 strands of light green tog as 1, join with sl st in any ch-5 sp, ch 1, sc in same ch sp, *ch 6, sl st in 2nd ch from hook, sc in next ch, dc in each of next 3 chs, sc in next ch-5 sp, ch 6**, sc in next ch-5 sp, rep from * around, ending last rep at **, join. Fasten off. ❑❑

Christmas Rose

SKILL LEVEL

INTERMEDIATE

FINISHED SIZE
13 Inches across

MATERIALS
❑ Crochet cotton size 10:
    200 yds ecru
    100 yds burgundy
❑ 25 yds gold lamé thread
❑ Size 6/1.80mm steel crochet hook or size needed to obtain gauge

GAUGE
Rnds 1–3 = 2 inches

SPECIAL STITCHES
Shell: (2 dc, ch 2, 2 dc) in next st or ch sp.

Picot: Ch 5, sl st in 3rd ch from hook, ch 2.

INSTRUCTIONS
ROSE
Make 8.

Rnd 1: With burgundy, wrap thread around finger twice to form a ring, ch 3 *(counts as first dc)*, 9 dc in ring, pull end of thread tightly to close ring, join with sl st in top of beg ch-3. *(10 dc)*

Rnd 2: Ch 1, sc in first st, sc in each st around, join with sl st in beg sc.

Rnd 3: Ch 1, sc in first st, ch 3, sk next st, [sc in next st, ch 3, sk next st] around, join.

Rnd 4: (Sl st, ch 3, 4 dc, ch 3, sl st) in first ch sp and in each ch sp around, **do not join.** *(5 petals)*

Rnd 5: Working behind petals, ch 1, [sc in ch-3 sp on rnd before last between center 2 dc of last rnd, ch 4] around, join with sl st in beg sc.

Rnd 6: (Sl st, ch 3, 6 dc, ch 3, sl st) in first ch-4 sp and in each ch-4 sp around, **do not join.**

Rnd 7: Working behind petals, ch 1, [sc in ch-4 sp on rnd before last between center 2 dc of last rnd, ch 5] around, join with sl st in beg sc.

Rnd 8: (Sl st, ch 3, 8 dc, ch 3, sl st) in first ch-5 sp and in each ch-5 sp around, join with sl st in beg sl st. Fasten off.
Set Roses aside to be joined later.

DOILY

Rnd 1: With ecru, wrap thread around finger twice to form a ring, ch 3 *(counts as first dc)*, 15 dc in ring, pull end of thread tightly to close ring, join with sl st in top of beg ch-3. *(16 dc)*

Rnd 2: Ch 3, dc in same st, 2 dc in each st around, join. *(32 dc)*

Rnd 3: Ch 3, 2 dc in next st, [dc in next st, 2 dc in next st] around, join. *(48 dc)*

Rnd 4: Ch 6 *(counts as first dc and ch 3)*, sk next st, [dc in next st, ch 3, sk next st] around, join with sl st in 3rd ch of beg ch-6.

Rnd 5: Ch 3, dc in each ch and in each st around, join with sl st in top of beg ch-3. *(96 dc)*

Rnd 6: Working in **back lps** *(see Stitch Guide)*, ch 3, dc in each st around, join.

Rnd 7: Ch 1, sc in first st, [ch 9, sk next 5 sts, sc in next st], around, join with ch 4, tr in beg sc forming last ch sp. *(16 ch-9 sps)*

Rnd 8: Ch 1, (sc, ch 3, sc) in last ch sp made, ch 9, [(sc, ch 3, sc) in center ch of next ch-9 sp, ch 9] around, join with sl st in beg sc.

Rnd 9: Sl st to ch-3 sp, ch 1, sc in same ch sp, *sc in first ch of next ch-9 sp, [ch 3, sk next ch, sc in next ch] 4 times**, sc in next ch-3 sp, rep from * around, ending last rep at **, join. Fasten off.

Rnd 10: Join ecru with sc in first ch-3 sp, *[ch 3, sc in next ch-3 sp] 3 times, ch 2**, sc in next ch-3 sp, rep from * around, ending last rep at **, join.

Rnd 11: Sl st in next ch-3 sp, ch 1, sc in same ch sp, *[ch 3, sc in next ch-3 sp] twice, ch 5, sk next ch-2 sp**, sc in next ch-3 sp, rep from * around, ending last rep at **, join.

Rnd 12: Sl st in next ch-3 sp, ch 1, sc in same ch sp, *ch 3, sc in next ch sp, working in next 5 chs, 2 dc in each of first 2 chs, dc in next ch, 2 dc in each of last 2 chs**, sc in next ch-3 sp, rep from * around, ending last rep at **, join.

Rnd 13: Sl st in next ch sp, (ch 3, dc, ch 2, 2 dc) in same ch sp, *ch 3, sk next 3 dc, sc in next dc, ch 1, sc between center 2 dc on 1 Rose, ch 1, sk next dc on Doily, sc in next dc, ch 3, sk next 3 dc, **shell** *(see Special Stitches)* in next ch-3 sp, ch 3, sk next 3 dc, sc in next dc, ch 3, sk next dc, sc in next dc, ch 3, sk next 3 dc**, shell in next ch-3 sp, rep from * around, ending last rep at **, join with sl st in beg ch-3.

Rnd 14: Sl st to ch sp of first shell, ch 5 *(counts as first dtr)*, dtr in same ch sp, *ch 3, (sc, ch 3, sc) between center 2 dc on next petal of Rose, [ch 11, (sc, ch 3, sc) between center 2 dc on next petal of Rose] 3 times, ch 3, 2 dtr in ch sp of next shell on Doily, ch 1,shell in next ch-3 sp, ch 1**, 2 dtr in ch sp of next shell, rep from * around, ending last rep at **, join with sl st in top of ch-5. Fasten off.

Rnd 15: Join with sl st in first ch-3 sp on first Rose, ch 1, sc in same ch sp, ◊*working across ch 11, sc in first ch [ch 3, sk next ch, sc in next ch] 5 times, sc in next ch 3 sp, rep from * twice, ch 5, shell in ch sp of next shell, ch 5**, sc in first ch-3 sp on next Rose, rep from ◊ around, ending last rep at **, join.

Rnd 16: Sl st in next ch-3 sp, ch 1, sc in same ch sp, *[ch 3, sc in next ch-3 sp] 4 times, ch 2, sc in next ch-3 sp, [ch 3, sc in next ch-3 sp] 4 times, ch 2, sc in next ch-3 sp, [ch 3, sc in next ch-3 sp] 4 times, ch 3, sc in next ch-5 sp, ch 5, sk shell, sc in next ch-5 sp, ch 3** sc in next ch-3 sp, rep from * around, ending last rep at **, join.

Rnd 17: Sl st in next ch-3 sp, ch 4 *(counts as first dc and ch-1)*, *(dc, ch 1) 3 times in same ch sp, dc in same ch sp, sc in next ch sp, ch 3, sc in next ch sp, dc in next ch sp, (ch 1, dc) 4 times in same ch sp, sc in next ch sp, dc in next ch sp, (ch 1, dc) 4 times in same ch sp, sc in next ch sp, **picot** *(see Special Stitches)*, sc in next ch sp, dc in next ch sp, (ch 1, dc) 4 times in same ch sp, sc in next ch sp, dc in next ch sp, (ch 1, dc) 4 times in same ch sp, sc in next ch sp, ch 3, sc in next ch sp, dc in next ch sp, (ch 1, dc) 4 times in same ch sp, ch 1, sc in next ch-5 sp, ch 1**, dc in next ch sp, rep from * around, ending last rep at **, join with sl st in 3rd ch of first ch-4. Fasten off.

RUFFLE

Rnd 1: Working in **front lps** *(see Stitch Guide)* of rnd 5 on Doily, join ecru with sl st in any st, ch 4 *(counts as dc and ch 1)*, (dc, ch 1, dc) in next st, ch 1, [dc in next st, ch 1, (dc, ch 1, dc) in next st, ch 1] around, join with sl st in 3rd ch of beg ch-4. *(120 dc)*

Rnd 2: Ch 4, [dc in next st, ch 1] around, join with sl st in 3rd ch of beg ch-4. Fasten off.

Rnd 3: Join gold lamé thread with sc in any ch sp, ch 4, [sc in next ch sp, ch 4] around, join with sl st in beg sc. Fasten off. ❑❑

SKILL LEVEL

INTERMEDIATE

FINISHED SIZE
13½ inches across

MATERIALS
❑ Crochet cotton size 10:
  200 yds ecru
  50 yds dark yellow
❑ 6-strand embroidery floss:
  75 yds dark brown
  50 yds dark green
❑ Size 6/1.80mm steel crochet hook or size needed to obtain gauge

GAUGE
Rnds 1–3 = 2 inches

INSTRUCTIONS
SUNFLOWER
Make 12.
Center
Rnd 1: With dark brown, wrap floss around finger twice to form a ring, ch 1, 8 sc in ring, pull end of thread tightly to close ring, join with sl st in beg sc. *(8 sc)*

Rnd 2: Ch 1, 2 sc in each st around, join. *(16 sc)*

Rnd 3: Ch 1, sc in each st around, join. Fasten off.

Petals
Join dark yellow with sl st in any sc on last rnd of Center, (ch 2, dc, ch 2, sl st in first ch from hook, dc, ch 2, sl st) in same st. ch 1, [sk next st, (sl st, ch 2, dc, ch 2, sl st in first ch from hook, dc, ch 2, sl st) in next st, ch 1] around, join with sl st in beg sl st. Fasten off.

Lay Sunflowers aside to be joined later.

DOILY
Rnd 1: With ecru, wrap thread around finger twice to form a ring, ch 3 *(counts as dc)*, 15 dc in ring, pull end of thread tightly to close ring, join with sl st in top of beg ch-3. *(16 dc)*

Rnd 2: Ch 3, dc in same st, 2 dc in

each st around, join. *(32 dc)*

Rnd 3: Ch 3, 2 dc in next st, [dc in next st, 2 dc in next st] around, join. *(48 dc)*

Rnd 4: Ch 3, dc in next st, 2 dc in next st, [dc in each of next 2 sts, 2 dc in next st] around, join *(64 dc)*

Rnd 5: Ch 3, dc in each of next 2 sts, 2 dc in next st, [dc in each of next 3 sts, 2 dc in next st] around, join. *(80 dc)*

Rnd 6: Working in **back lps** *(see Stitch Guide)*, ch 3, dc in each of next 2 sts, 2 dc in next st, [dc in each of next 3 sts, 2 dc in next st] around, join. *(100 dc)*

Rnd 7: Ch 1, sc in first st, [ch 3, sk next st, sc in next st] around, sk last st, join with dc in beg sc to form last ch sp.

Rnd 8: Ch 1, sc in last ch sp made, [ch 4, sc in next ch sp] around, join with ch 1, dc in beg sc to form last ch sp.

Rnd 9: Ch 1, sc in last ch sp made, [ch 4, sc in next ch sp] around, join with ch 1, dc in beg sc to form last ch sp.

Rnd 10: Ch 1, sc in last ch sp made, [ch 4, sc in next ch sp] around, join with ch 1, dc in beg sc to form last ch sp.

Rnd 11: Ch 1, sc in last ch sp made, [ch 5, sc in next ch sp] around, join with ch 2, dc in beg sc to form last ch sp.

Rnd 12: Ch 1, sc in last ch sp made, [ch 5, sc in next ch sp] around, join with ch 2, dc in beg sc to form last ch sp.

Rnd 13: Ch 1, sc in last ch sp made, [ch 5, sc in next ch sp] around, join with ch 2, dc in beg sc to form last ch sp.

Rnd 14: Ch 4 *(counts as first tr)*, tr in same ch sp, ch 3, [2 tr in next ch sp, ch 3] around, join with sl st in top of beg ch-4. Fasten off.

Rnd 15: Join dark green floss with sc in sp between first and 2nd tr, *ch 5, sl st in 2nd ch from hook, sc in next ch, dc in each of next 2 chs, sc in next ch-3 sp, ch 5, sl st in 2nd ch from hook, sc in next ch, dc in each of next 2 chs, sc in sp between next 2 tr**, [ch 5, sc in sp between next 2 tr] twice, rep from * around, ending last rep at **, ch 5, sc in sp between next 2 tr, ch 5, join with sl st in beg sc. Fasten off.

SUNFLOWER JOINING

Rnd 16: Join ecru with sl st in next ch-5 sp, ch 1, sc in same ch sp, *ch 2, sl st in any ch-1 sp between petals on 1 Sunflower, ch 2, sc in same ch-5 sp on Doily, ch 7, (dc, ch 3, dc) in each of next 2 ch-5 sps, ch 7**, sc in next ch-5 sp, rep from * around, ending last rep at **, join with sl st in beg sc. Fasten off.

Rnd 17: Sk next 2 petals to the left of last joining on first Sunflower, join ecru with sl st in next ch-1 sp between petals, *ch 3, (sc, ch 3, sc) in center ch of next ch-7 sp on Doily, [ch 5, sc in next ch-3 sp] twice, ch 5, (sc, ch 3, sc) in center ch of next ch-7 sp, sk next 2 petals on next Sunflower**, [ch 5, sl st in next ch-1 sp on same Sunflower] 5 times, rep from * around, ending last rep at **, [ch 5, sl st in next ch-1 sp on same Sunflower] 4 times, join with ch 2, dc in beg sl st forming last ch sp.

Rnd 18: Ch 1, sc in last ch sp made, *ch 4, sk next ch-5 sp, (2 dc, ch 3, 2 dc) in center ch of next ch-5 sp, ch 4, sk next ch-5 sp, sc in next ch-5 sp**, [ch 6, sc in next ch-5 sp] 3 times, rep from * around, ending last rep at **, [ch 6, sc in next ch-5 sp] twice, ch 6, join with sl st in beg sc.

Rnd 19: *Ch 5, working over ch-4 of last rnd, sc in sk ch-5 sp of last rnd, 7 dc in next ch-3 sp, sc in next sk ch-5 sp of last rnd, ch 5, [working in chs of next ch-6, sc in first ch, dc in next ch, 2 tr in each of next 2 chs, dc in next ch, sc in last ch] 3 times, rep from * around, join with sl st in first ch of beg ch-5. Fasten off.

Rnd 20: Join dark green floss with sc in center ch of first ch-5 sp, ch 3, sc in same ch, *ch 3, (sc, ch 3, sc) in center dc of next dc group, ch 3, (sc, ch 3, sc) in center ch of next ch-5 sp, ch 3, sl st in next st, [ch 1, sl st in next st] across to next ch-5 sp, ch 3**, (sc, ch 3, sc) in center ch of ch-5 sp, rep from * around, ending last rep at **, join with sl st in beg sc. Fasten off.

RUFFLE

Rnd 1: Working in **front lps** (See Stitch Guide) of rnd 5 on Doily, join ecru with sl st in any st, ch 5 (counts as tr and ch 1), (tr, ch 1, tr) in next st, ch 1, [tr in next st, ch 1, (tr, ch 1, tr) in next st, ch 1] around, join with sl st in 4th ch of beg ch-5. (120 tr)

Rnd 2: Ch 5, [tr in next st, ch 1] around, join with sl st in 4th ch of beg ch-5. Fasten off.

Rnd 3: Join dark green floss with sc in any ch sp, ch 3, [sc in next ch sp, ch 3] around, join with sl st in beg sc. Fasten off. ❏❏

Daisies

SKILL LEVEL
INTERMEDIATE

FINISHED SIZE
12½ inches across

MATERIALS
- ❑ Crochet cotton size 10:
  - 100 yds ecru
  - 50 yds light yellow
  - 30 yds light green
  - 20 yds dark yellow
- ❑ Size 6/1.80mm steel crochet hook or size needed to obtain gauge

GAUGE
Rnds 1–3 = 2 inches

SPECIAL STITCHES
Beginning popcorn (beg pc): Ch 3, 3 dc in same st or ch sp, drop lp from hook, insert hook in top of ch 3, pull dropped lp through.

Popcorn (pc): 4 dc in st or ch sp, drop lp from hook, insert hook in top of first dc of group, pull dropped lp through.

Picot: Ch 3, sl st in 3rd ch from hook, ch 1.

INSTRUCTIONS
DOILY
Rnd 1: With ecru, wrap thread around finger twice to form a ring, ch 3 *(counts as dc)*, 15 dc in ring, pull end of thread tightly to close ring, join with sl st in top of beg ch-3. *(16 dc)*

Rnd 2: Ch 3, dc in same st, 2 dc in each st around, join. *(32 dc)*

Rnd 3: Ch 3, 2 dc in next st, [dc in next st, 2 dc in next st] around, join. *(48 dc)*

Rnd 4: Ch 3, dc in next st, 2 dc in next st, [dc in each of next 2 sts, 2 dc in next st] around, join *(64 dc)*

Rnd 5: Ch 3, dc in each of next 2 sts, 2 dc in next st, [dc in each of next 3 sts, 2 dc in next st] around, join. *(80 dc)*

Rnd 6: Ch 1, sc in first st, [ch 3, sk next st, sc in next st] around, join with dc in beg sc forming last ch sp. *(40 ch sps)*

Rnd 7: Ch 1, sc in ch sp just made, [ch 3, sc in next ch sp] around, join with dc in beg sc.

Rnd 8: Beg pc *(see Special Stitches)* in ch sp just made, [ch 4, **pc** *(see Special Stitches)* in next ch sp] around, join with ch 1, dc in top of beg pc.

Rnd 9: Ch 1, sc in ch sp just made, [ch 5, sc in next ch sp] around, join with ch 2, dc in beg sc.

Rnd 10: Ch 1, sc in ch sp just made, ch 5, [sc in next ch sp, ch 5] around, join with sl st in beg sc. Fasten off.

FIRST DAISY MOTIF
Rnd 1: With dark yellow, wrap thread around finger twice to form a ring, ch 1, 8 sc in ring, pull end of thread tightly to close ring, join with sl st in beg sc. *(8 sc)*

Rnds 2–4: Ch 1, sc in each st around, join. At end of last rnd, fasten off.

Petals
Rnd 5: Join light yellow with sl st in first st, beg pc in same st, ch 1, pc in same st, ch 1, (pc, ch 1, pc, ch 1) in each st around, join with sl st to top of beg pc. Fasten off.

Leaves
Rnd 6: Join light green with sl st in any ch-1 sp between Petals, ch 1, sc in same ch sp, *ch 3, sc in next ch sp, ch 4, sl st in 2nd ch from hook, sc in next ch, hdc in last ch**, sc in next ch-1 sp, rep from * around, ending last rep at **, join with sl st in beg sc. Fasten off.

Joining

Rnd 7: Join ecru with sl st in any ch 3 sp, ch 1, (sc, ch 3, sc) in same ch sp, [ch-5, (sc, ch 3, sc) in next ch sp] around, join with ch 2, dc in beg sc *(last ch sp made)*.

Rnd 8: Ch 1, sc in ch sp just made, [ch 2, sc in ch-5 sp on Doily, ch 2, sc in next ch sp on Daisy Motif] twice, ch 5, [sc in next ch sp, ch 5] around, join with sl st in beg sc. Fasten off.

JOINED DAISY MOTIF
Make 7.

Rnds 1–7: Work same as rnds 1–7 of First Daisy Motif.

Rnd 8: Ch 1, sc in ch sp just made, sk next 3 ch sps on Doily, [ch 2, sc in next ch-5 sp on Doily, ch 2, sc in next ch sp on this Motif] twice, [ch 5, sc in next ch sp on this Motif] twice, sk 2 ch sps on last Daisy Motif, [ch 2, sc in next ch sp on last Daisy Motif, ch 2, sc in next ch sp on this Motif]

twice, ch 5, [sc in next ch sp on this Motif, ch 5] around, join with sl st in beg sc. Fasten off.

LAST DAISY MOTIF

Rnds 1–7: Work same as rnds 1–7 of First Daisy Motif.

Rnd 8: Ch 1, sc in ch sp just formed, sk next 3 ch sps on Doily, [ch 2, sc in next ch-5 sp on Doily, ch 2, sc in next ch sp on this Motif] twice, [ch 5, sc in next ch sp on this Motif] twice, sk next 2 ch sps on last Daisy Motif, [ch 2, sc in next ch sp on last Daisy Motif, ch 2, sc in next ch sp on this Motif] twice, [ch 5, sc in next ch sp on this Motif] 6 times, sk next 2 ch sps from joining to Doily on First Daisy Motif, [ch 2, sc in next ch sp on last Daisy Motif, ch 2, sc in next ch sp on this Motif] twice, ch 5, sc in next ch sp, ch 5, join with sl st in beg sc. Fasten off.

EDGING

Rnd 1: Join ecru with sl st in first unjoined ch-5 sp to left of joining on Motif, ch 1, sc in same ch sp, working in unworked ch-5 sps, ch 6, [sc in next ch sp, ch 6] around, join with sl st in beg sc.

Rnd 2: Sl st in ch sp, ch 6, sl st in 3rd ch from hook, ch 1, (dc, **picot**—*see Special Stitches*) 5 times in same ch sp as sl st, *sc in next ch sp, ch 1**, (dc, picot) 6 times in next ch sp, rep from * around, ending last rep at **, join with sl st in 3rd ch of beg ch-6. Fasten off.

RUFFLE

Working in **front lps** *(see Stitch Guide)* of sk sts on rnd 5, join ecru with sl st in first st past joining, ch 3, 5 dc in same st, sc in next st, [6 dc in next st, sc in next st] around, join with sl st in top of beg ch-3. Fasten off. ❏❏

Lilacs & Lace

SKILL LEVEL

INTERMEDIATE

FINISHED SIZE
10½ inches across

MATERIALS
- ❏ Crochet cotton size 10:
    - 100 yds ecru
    - 25 yds lilac
    - 15 yds light green
- ❏ Size 6/1.80mm steel crochet hook or size needed to obtain gauge
- ❏ 10 ivory size 3mm beads
- ❏ Glue gun

GAUGE
Rnds 1–3 = 2 inches

INSTRUCTIONS
DOILY
Rnd 1: With ecru, wrap thread around finger twice to form a ring, ch 3 *(counts as dc)*, 15 dc in ring, pull end of thread tightly to close ring, join with sl st in top of beg ch-3. *(16 dc)*

Rnd 2: Ch 3, dc in same st, 2 dc in each st around, join. *(32 dc)*

Rnd 3: Ch 3, 2 dc in next st, [dc in next st, 2 dc in next st] around, join. *(48 dc)*

Rnd 4: Ch 3, dc in next st, 2 dc in next st, [dc in each of next 2 sts, 2 dc in next st] around, join *(64 dc)*

Rnd 5: Ch 3, dc in each of next 2 sts, 2 dc in next st, [dc in each of next 3 sts, 2 dc in next st] around, join. *(80 dc)*

Rnd 6: Working in **back lps** *(see Stitch Guide)*, ch 1, sc in first st, [ch 3, sk next st, sc in next st] around, sk last st, join with dc in beg sc to forming last ch sp. *(40 ch sps)*

Rnd 7: Ch 1, sc in last ch sp made, [ch 4, sc in next ch sp] around, join with ch 1, dc in beg sc forming last ch sp.

Rnd 8: Ch 1, sc in last ch sp just made, [ch 4, sc in next ch sp] around, join with ch 1, dc in beg sc forming last ch sp.

Rnd 9: Ch 1, sc in last ch sp just made, [ch 5, sc in next ch sp] around, join with ch 2, dc in beg sc forming last ch sp.

Rnd 10: Ch 1, sc in last ch sp just made, [ch 5, sc in next ch sp] around, join with ch 2, dc in beg sc forming last ch sp.

Rnd 11: Ch 1, (sc, ch 3, sc) in last ch sp just made, ch 13, sk next ch sp, [(sc, ch 3, sc) in next ch sp, ch 13, sk next ch sp] around, join with sl st in beg sc. Fasten off.

Rnd 12: Join ecru with sl st in 4th ch of first ch-13, ch 3, dc in same ch, *dc in next ch, 2 dc in next ch, (dc, ch 3, dc) in next ch, 2 dc in next ch, dc in next ch, 2 dc in next ch**, 2 dc in 4th ch of next ch-13, rep from * around, ending last rep at **, join with sl st in top of beg ch-3.

Rnd 13: Sl st across to first ch-3 sp, ch 1, (sc, ch 3, sc) in same ch-3 sp, *ch 7, sk next 6 sts, sc in sp between dc groups**, ch 7, (sc, ch 3, sc) in next ch-3 sp, rep from * around, ending last rep at **, join with ch 3, tr in beg sc forming last ch sp.

Rnd 14: Ch 1, (sc, ch 3, sc) in last ch sp made, *ch 7, (sc, ch 3, sc) in next ch sp**, ch 5, (sc, ch 3, sc) in next ch sp, rep from * around, ending last rep at **, join with ch 2, dc in beg sc to form last ch sp.

Rnd 15: Ch 1, (sc, ch 3, sc) in last ch sp made, *ch 1, dc in first ch of next ch-7, ch 1, 2 dc in next ch, ch 1, [dc in next ch, ch 1] 3 times, 2 dc in next ch, ch 1, dc in last ch, ch 1**, (sc, ch 3, sc) in center ch of next ch-5 sp, rep from * around, ending last rep at **, join with sl st in beg sc.

Rnd 16: Sl st in first ch-3 sp, ch 1, sc in same ch sp, *sk next ch-1 sp, sc in next ch-1 sp, [ch 3, sc in next ch-1 sp] 7 times**, sc in next ch-3 sp, rep from * around, ending last rep at **, join with sl st in beg sc. Fasten off.

RUFFLE

Rnd 1: Working in **front lps** *(see Stitch Guide)* of rnd 5, join ecru with sl st in 2nd st, ch 4 *(counts as first dc and ch 1)*, (dc, ch 1) 3 times in same st, sk next st, [(dc, ch 1) 4 times in next st, sk next st] around, join with sl st in 3rd ch of beg ch-4.

Rnd 2: Ch 5 *(counts as first dc and ch-2)*, [dc in next st, ch 2] around, join with sl st in 3rd ch of beg ch-5. Fasten off.

Rnd 3: Join light green with sc in any ch-2 sp, ch 4, [sc in next ch sp, ch 4] around, join with sl st in beg sc. Fasten off.

LILACS
Make 10.

Form ring with lilac, (sl st, ch 2, 2 dc, ch 2, sl st) 5 times in ring, pull end of thread tightly to close ring join with sl st in beg sl st. Fasten off.

LEAVES
Make 10.

With light green, [ch 6, sl st in 2nd ch from hook, sc in next ch, hdc in next ch, dc in each of last 2 chs] twice. Fasten off.

FINISHING

1. With glue gun, glue 1 set of Leaves to each Lilac.

2. Glue Lilacs to Doily as shown in photo.

3. Glue 1 bead to center of each Lilac. ❏❏

Stitch Guide

ABBREVIATIONS

beg	begin/beginning
bpdc	back post double crochet
bpsc	back post single crochet
bptr	back post treble crochet
CC	contrasting color
ch	chain stitch
ch-	refers to chain or space previously made (i.e. ch-1 space)
ch sp	chain space
cl	cluster
cm	centimeter(s)
dc	double crochet
dec	decrease/decreases/decreasing
dtr	double treble crochet
fpdc	front post double crochet
fpsc	front post single crochet
fptr	front post treble crochet
g	gram(s)
hdc	half double crochet
inc	increase/increases/increasing
lp(s)	loop(s)
MC	main color
mm	millimeter(s)
oz	ounce(s)
pc	popcorn
rem	remain/remaining
rep	repeat(s)
rnd(s)	round(s)
RS	right side
sc	single crochet
sk	skip(ped)
sl st	slip stitch
sp(s)	space(s)
st(s)	stitch(es)
tog	together
tr	treble crochet
trtr	triple treble
WS	wrong side
yd(s)	yard(s)
yo	yarn over

Chain—ch: Yo, pull through lp on hook.

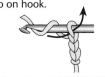

Slip stitch—sl st: Insert hook in st, yo, pull through both lps on hook.

Single crochet—sc: Insert hook in st, yo, pull through st, yo, pull through both lps on hook.

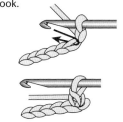

Front loop—front lp
Back loop—back lp

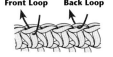

Front Loop   Back Loop

Front post stitch—fp: Back post stitch—bp: When working post st, insert hook from right to left around post st on previous row.

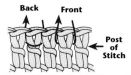

Back   Front

Post of Stitch

Half double crochet—hdc: Yo, insert hook in st, yo, pull through st, yo, pull through all 3 lps on hook.

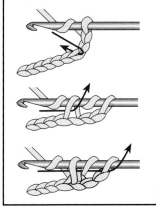

Double crochet—dc: Yo, insert hook in st, yo, pull through st, [yo, pull through 2 lps] twice.

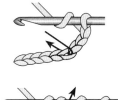

Change colors: Drop first color; with second color, pull through last 2 lps of st.

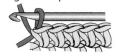

Treble crochet—tr: Yo twice, insert hook in st, yo, pull through st, [yo, pull through 2 lps] 3 times.

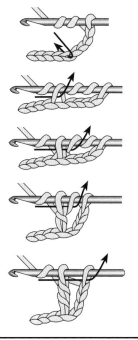

Double treble crochet—dtr: Yo 3 times, insert hook in st, yo, pull through st, [yo, pull through 2 lps] 4 times.

Single crochet decrease (sc dec): (Insert hook, yo, draw up a lp) in each of the sts indicated, yo, draw through all lps on hook.

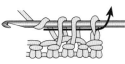

Example of 2-sc dec

Half double crochet decrease (hdc dec): (Yo, insert hook, yo, draw lp through) in each of the sts indicated, yo, draw through all lps on hook.

Example of 2-hdc dec

Double crochet decrease (dc dec): (Yo, insert hook, yo, draw lp through, yo, draw through 2 lps on hook) in each of the sts indicated, yo, draw through all lps on hook.

Example of 2-dc dec

US		UK
sl st (slip stitch)	=	sc (single crochet)
sc (single crochet)	=	dc (double crochet)
hdc (half double crochet)	=	htr (half treble crochet)
dc (double crochet)	=	tr (treble crochet)
tr (treble crochet)	=	dtr (double treble crochet)
dtr (double treble crochet)	=	ttr (triple treble crochet)
skip	=	miss

For more complete information, visit

StitchGuide.com

306 East Parr Road
Berne, IN 46711
© 2005 Annie's Attic

TOLL-FREE ORDER LINE or to request a free catalog (800) LV-ANNIE (800) 582-6643
Customer Service (800) AT-ANNIE (800) 282-6643, **Fax** (800) 882-6643
Visit www.AnniesAttic.com

ISBN: 1-59635-029-6
Printed in USA
1 2 3 4 5 6 7 8 9